HOW CAN THIS BOOK HELP YOU?

Hello!

Thank you for purchasing this revision book.

Creative writing can be a captivating journey of self-expression and literary exploration. It's not just an essential component of the English Language exam; it's an art form that allows you to paint vivid stories, evoke emotions, and share your imagination with the world. The ability to craft compelling narratives, paint scenes with words, and wield the power of storytelling is an invaluable skill that can open doors in your academic journey and beyond.

In my experience as a secondary school English teacher and tutor, as well as having completed my university degree in English and Creative Writing, I can confidently say that the best way to get better (and get better quickly) at creative writing is by…well…WRITING! The more you write, the better you'll understand what works for you and what doesn't, where your areas of strength are and where you need to improve, and, perhaps most critically, you'll begin to develop your own voice.

That's where this book comes in. I have put together 50 original creative writing questions for you to use as prompts for practising your own craft. Some of the prompts you'll find straightforward and others you'll find more challenging due to their abstract nature – my advice is to have a go at as many as you can, because if you can conquer the difficult practice questions then you'll be unstoppable when the exam finally comes around.

Happy Writing!
Mr Watson

PRACTICE QUESTION 1

You are advised to spend about 45 minutes on this section.
Write in full sentences.
You are reminded of the need to plan your answer.
You should leave enough time to check your work at the end.

A website has asked for examples of creating writing for its new page.

EITHER: Write a description as suggested by this picture.

OR: Write a story about a time you were surprised.

24 marks for content and organisation
16 marks for technical accuracy
(40 marks)

PRACTICE QUESTION 2

> You are advised to spend about 45 minutes on this section.
> Write in full sentences.
> You are reminded of the need to plan your answer.
> You should leave enough time to check your work at the end.

A creative writing website is seeking submissions for its new collection.

EITHER: Write a description as suggested by this picture.

OR: Write a story about an adventure.

24 marks for content and organisation
16 marks for technical accuracy
(40 marks)

3

PRACTICE QUESTION 3

> You are advised to spend about 45 minutes on this section.
> Write in full sentences.
> You are reminded of the need to plan your answer.
> You should leave enough time to check your work at the end.

A creative writing blog has asked for examples of creative writing for its upcoming feature.

EITHER: Write a description as suggested by this picture.

OR: Write a story about a celebration.

24 marks for content and organisation
16 marks for technical accuracy
(40 marks)

PRACTICE QUESTION 4

You are advised to spend about 45 minutes on this section.
Write in full sentences.
You are reminded of the need to plan your answer.
You should leave enough time to check your work at the end.

A website has asked for examples of creating writing for its new page.

EITHER: Write a description as suggested by this picture.

OR: Write the opening of a story that begins: "They could hear the rain bombarding the street outside."

24 marks for content and organisation
16 marks for technical accuracy
(40 marks)

PRACTICE QUESTION 5

You are advised to spend about 45 minutes on this section.
Write in full sentences.
You are reminded of the need to plan your answer.
You should leave enough time to check your work at the end.

A creative writing blog has asked for examples of creative writing for its upcoming feature.

EITHER: Write a description as suggested by this picture.

OR: Write the opening of a story that begins: "I had become lost in the crowd once again."

24 marks for content and organisation
16 marks for technical accuracy
(40 marks)

6

PRACTICE QUESTION 6

You are advised to spend about 45 minutes on this section.
Write in full sentences.
You are reminded of the need to plan your answer.
You should leave enough time to check your work at the end.

A fiction magazine is looking for creative writing submissions to publish in its next issue.

EITHER: Write a description as suggested by this picture.

OR: Write the opening of a story that begins: "Everything happens for a reason."

24 marks for content and organisation
16 marks for technical accuracy
(40 marks)

PRACTICE QUESTION 7

You are advised to spend about 45 minutes on this section.
Write in full sentences.
You are reminded of the need to plan your answer.
You should leave enough time to check your work at the end.

Your school is asking students to contribute some creating writing for its website.

EITHER: Write a description as suggested by this picture.

OR: Write a short story based around a memory.

24 marks for content and organisation
16 marks for technical accuracy
(40 marks)

PRACTICE QUESTION 8

You are advised to spend about 45 minutes on this section.
Write in full sentences.
You are reminded of the need to plan your answer.
You should leave enough time to check your work at the end.

Your headteacher wants you to contribute a piece of creating writing for the school newsletter.

EITHER: Write a story about a great journey as suggested by this picture.

OR: Write a description about a place that has had a lasting impression on you.

24 marks for content and organisation
16 marks for technical accuracy
(40 marks)

PRACTICE QUESTION 9

You are advised to spend about 45 minutes on this section.
Write in full sentences.
You are reminded of the need to plan your answer.
You should leave enough time to check your work at the end.

A creative writing platform is actively seeking submissions of creative writing for its showcase.

EITHER: Write a description as suggested by this picture.

OR: Write a short story about a peaceful place.

24 marks for content and organisation
16 marks for technical accuracy
(40 marks)

PRACTICE QUESTION 10

You are advised to spend about 45 minutes on this section.
Write in full sentences.
You are reminded of the need to plan your answer.
You should leave enough time to check your work at the end.

A literary website is currently looking for examples of creative writing for its featured section.

EITHER: Write a description as suggested by this picture.

OR: Write a short story that begins: "There was nobody left."

24 marks for content and organisation
16 marks for technical accuracy
(40 marks)

PRACTICE QUESTION 11

You are advised to spend about 45 minutes on this section.
Write in full sentences.
You are reminded of the need to plan your answer.
You should leave enough time to check your work at the end.

A well-known magazine has asked for creative writing pieces for its monthly publication.

EITHER: Write a short story about a city as suggested by this picture.

OR: Write a description about a place from history.

24 marks for content and organisation
16 marks for technical accuracy
(40 marks)

PRACTICE QUESTION 12

> You are advised to spend about 45 minutes on this section.
> Write in full sentences.
> You are reminded of the need to plan your answer.
> You should leave enough time to check your work at the end.

An online writing blog is currently looking for examples of creative writing for its feed.

EITHER: Write a description as suggested by this picture.

OR: Write the opening of a short story about escaping the mundane.

24 marks for content and organisation
16 marks for technical accuracy
(40 marks)

13

PRACTICE QUESTION 13

You are advised to spend about 45 minutes on this section.
Write in full sentences.
You are reminded of the need to plan your answer.
You should leave enough time to check your work at the end.

A creative writing blog has asked for examples of creative writing for its upcoming feature.

EITHER: Write a description as suggested by this picture.

OR: Write the opening of a short story about a familiar place.

24 marks for content and organisation
16 marks for technical accuracy
(40 marks)

PRACTICE QUESTION 14

You are advised to spend about 45 minutes on this section.
Write in full sentences.
You are reminded of the need to plan your answer.
You should leave enough time to check your work at the end.

A fiction magazine is looking for creative writing submissions to publish in its next issue.

EITHER: Write a short story as suggested by this picture.

OR: Write a description about a journey.

24 marks for content and organisation
16 marks for technical accuracy
(40 marks)

15

PRACTICE QUESTION 15

You are advised to spend about 45 minutes on this section.
Write in full sentences.
You are reminded of the need to plan your answer.
You should leave enough time to check your work at the end.

Your school is asking students to contribute some creating writing for its website.

EITHER: Write a description as suggested by this picture.

OR: Write the opening of a short story about a mysterious island.

24 marks for content and organisation
16 marks for technical accuracy
(40 marks)

PRACTICE QUESTION 16

You are advised to spend about 45 minutes on this section.
Write in full sentences.
You are reminded of the need to plan your answer.
You should leave enough time to check your work at the end.

A creative writing competition is currently looking for examples of creative writing for its annual contest.

EITHER: Write a short story as suggested by this picture.

OR: Write a description about a time you had to wait.

24 marks for content and organisation
16 marks for technical accuracy
(40 marks)

17

PRACTICE QUESTION 17

You are advised to spend about 45 minutes on this section.
Write in full sentences.
You are reminded of the need to plan your answer.
You should leave enough time to check your work at the end.

Your school has asked for creative writing pieces for its literary magazine.

EITHER: Write a short story as suggested by this picture.

OR: Write a description about a place in nature.

24 marks for content and organisation
16 marks for technical accuracy
(40 marks)

PRACTICE QUESTION 18

You are advised to spend about 45 minutes on this section.
Write in full sentences.
You are reminded of the need to plan your answer.
You should leave enough time to check your work at the end.

A creative writing website has contacted you about submitting a piece of work to their site.

EITHER: Write a description as suggested by this picture.

OR: Write the opening to a story that begins: "At long last, there was peace."

24 marks for content and organisation
16 marks for technical accuracy
(40 marks)

19

PRACTICE QUESTION 19

You are advised to spend about 45 minutes on this section.
Write in full sentences.
You are reminded of the need to plan your answer.
You should leave enough time to check your work at the end.

Your teacher has asked you to produce a piece of creative writing.

EITHER: Write a description as suggested by this picture.

OR: Write a short story about a difficult choice.

24 marks for content and organisation
16 marks for technical accuracy
(40 marks)

PRACTICE QUESTION 20

> You are advised to spend about 45 minutes on this section.
> Write in full sentences.
> You are reminded of the need to plan your answer.
> You should leave enough time to check your work at the end.

A fiction magazine is looking for creative writing submissions to publish in its next issue.

EITHER: Write a short story as suggested by this picture.

OR: Write a description about a lonely place.

24 marks for content and organisation
16 marks for technical accuracy
(40 marks)

PRACTICE QUESTION 21

You are advised to spend about 45 minutes on this section.
Write in full sentences.
You are reminded of the need to plan your answer.
You should leave enough time to check your work at the end.

A creative writing blog has asked for creative writing submissions for its user-generated stories.

EITHER: Write a description as suggested by this picture.

OR: Write a short story about a holiday.

24 marks for content and organisation
16 marks for technical accuracy
(40 marks)

22

PRACTICE QUESTION 22

You are advised to spend about 45 minutes on this section.
Write in full sentences.
You are reminded of the need to plan your answer.
You should leave enough time to check your work at the end.

Your school is asking students to contribute some creative writing for its website.

EITHER: Write a description as suggested by this picture.

OR: Write a short story opening that beings: "There was a chill in the air that night."

24 marks for content and organisation
16 marks for technical accuracy
(40 marks)

PRACTICE QUESTION 23

You are advised to spend about 45 minutes on this section.
Write in full sentences.
You are reminded of the need to plan your answer.
You should leave enough time to check your work at the end.

A website has asked for examples of creating writing for its new page.

EITHER: Write a short story as suggested by this picture.

OR: Write a description of an epic moment.

24 marks for content and organisation
16 marks for technical accuracy
(40 marks)

PRACTICE QUESTION 24

You are advised to spend about 45 minutes on this section.
Write in full sentences.
You are reminded of the need to plan your answer.
You should leave enough time to check your work at the end.

Your headteacher wants you to contribute a piece of creating writing for the school newsletter.

EITHER: Write a description as suggested by this picture.

OR: Write a short story about being stuck.

24 marks for content and organisation
16 marks for technical accuracy
(40 marks)

PRACTICE QUESTION 25

You are advised to spend about 45 minutes on this section.
Write in full sentences.
You are reminded of the need to plan your answer.
You should leave enough time to check your work at the end.

Your headteacher wants you to contribute a piece of creating writing for the school newsletter.

EITHER: Write a description as suggested by this picture.

OR: Write the opening to a story about visiting a new place.

24 marks for content and organisation
16 marks for technical accuracy
(40 marks)

26

PRACTICE QUESTION 26

You are advised to spend about 45 minutes on this section.
Write in full sentences.
You are reminded of the need to plan your answer.
You should leave enough time to check your work at the end.

A website has asked for examples of creating writing for its new page.

EITHER: Write a description as suggested by this picture.

OR: Write the opening to a story which begins: "It wouldn't be long now."

24 marks for content and organisation
16 marks for technical accuracy
(40 marks)

27

PRACTICE QUESTION 27

You are advised to spend about 45 minutes on this section.
Write in full sentences.
You are reminded of the need to plan your answer.
You should leave enough time to check your work at the end.

A local writing group are looking for pieces of creative writing to showcase at the town hall.

EITHER: Write a short story as suggested by this picture.

OR: Write a description about a time you felt excited.

24 marks for content and organisation
16 marks for technical accuracy
(40 marks)

PRACTICE QUESTION 28

You are advised to spend about 45 minutes on this section.
Write in full sentences.
You are reminded of the need to plan your answer.
You should leave enough time to check your work at the end.

Your teacher has asked you to produce a piece of creative writing.

EITHER: Write a short story as suggested by this picture.

OR: Write a description about a time you were in awe.

24 marks for content and organisation
16 marks for technical accuracy
(40 marks)

PRACTICE QUESTION 29

> You are advised to spend about 45 minutes on this section.
> Write in full sentences.
> You are reminded of the need to plan your answer.
> You should leave enough time to check your work at the end.

A national writing publication is searching for examples of creative writing.

EITHER: Write a description as suggested by this picture.

OR: Write a short story about hope.

24 marks for content and organisation
16 marks for technical accuracy
(40 marks)

30

PRACTICE QUESTION 30

You are advised to spend about 45 minutes on this section.
Write in full sentences.
You are reminded of the need to plan your answer.
You should leave enough time to check your work at the end.

Your school is holding a creative writing contest.

EITHER: Write a description as suggested by this picture.

OR: Write the opening to a short story that begins: "You could cut the tension with a knife."

24 marks for content and organisation
16 marks for technical accuracy
(40 marks)

PRACTICE QUESTION 31

You are advised to spend about 45 minutes on this section.
Write in full sentences.
You are reminded of the need to plan your answer.
You should leave enough time to check your work at the end.

A local newspaper is searching for talented writers to feature in their upcoming issue.

EITHER: Write a description as suggested by this picture.

OR: Write the opening to a short story that begins: "It was far from an ordinary day."

24 marks for content and organisation
16 marks for technical accuracy
(40 marks)

PRACTICE QUESTION 32

> You are advised to spend about 45 minutes on this section.
> Write in full sentences.
> You are reminded of the need to plan your answer.
> You should leave enough time to check your work at the end.

Your school is requesting submissions for the upcoming creative writing newsletter.

EITHER: Write a description as suggested by this picture.

OR: Write the opening to a short story about love.

24 marks for content and organisation
16 marks for technical accuracy
(40 marks)

PRACTICE QUESTION 33

You are advised to spend about 45 minutes on this section.
Write in full sentences.
You are reminded of the need to plan your answer.
You should leave enough time to check your work at the end.

A website has asked for examples of creative writing for its new page.

EITHER: Write a description as suggested by this picture.

OR: Write the opening to a short story about friendship.

24 marks for content and organisation
16 marks for technical accuracy
(40 marks)

PRACTICE QUESTION 34

> You are advised to spend about 45 minutes on this section.
> Write in full sentences.
> You are reminded of the need to plan your answer.
> You should leave enough time to check your work at the end.

Your school wants you to contribute to a collection of creative writing.

EITHER: Write a description as suggested by this picture.

OR: Write the opening to a short story that begins: "The sun was setting on another day."

24 marks for content and organisation
16 marks for technical accuracy
(40 marks)

PRACTICE QUESTION 35

You are advised to spend about 45 minutes on this section.
Write in full sentences.
You are reminded of the need to plan your answer.
You should leave enough time to check your work at the end.

Your school is holding a creative writing competition and will publish the winning entries in the school magazine.

EITHER: Write a description as suggested by this picture.

OR: Write the opening to a short story about new beginnings.

24 marks for content and organisation
16 marks for technical accuracy
(40 marks)

PRACTICE QUESTION 36

You are advised to spend about 45 minutes on this section.
Write in full sentences.
You are reminded of the need to plan your answer.
You should leave enough time to check your work at the end.

A local magazine will be publishing creative writing pieces written by students.

EITHER: Write a description as suggested by this picture.

OR: Write the opening to a short story about struggle.

24 marks for content and organisation
16 marks for technical accuracy
(40 marks)

PRACTICE QUESTION 37

You are advised to spend about 45 minutes on this section.
Write in full sentences.
You are reminded of the need to plan your answer.
You should leave enough time to check your work at the end.

You are going to enter a creative writing competition for young people.

EITHER: Write the opening to a short story as suggested by this picture.

OR: Write a description about a thrilling experience.

24 marks for content and organisation
16 marks for technical accuracy
(40 marks)

PRACTICE QUESTION 38

You are advised to spend about 45 minutes on this section.
Write in full sentences.
You are reminded of the need to plan your answer.
You should leave enough time to check your work at the end.

A website has asked for contributions to its writing section.

EITHER: Write a description as suggested by this picture.

OR: Write a short story about a new start.

24 marks for content and organisation
16 marks for technical accuracy
(40 marks)

PRACTICE QUESTION 39

You are advised to spend about 45 minutes on this section.
Write in full sentences.
You are reminded of the need to plan your answer.
You should leave enough time to check your work at the end.

A local newspaper is looking for submissions for its creative writing section.

EITHER: Write a description as suggested by this picture.

OR: Write the opening to a short story that begins: "Another loss.".

24 marks for content and organisation
16 marks for technical accuracy
(40 marks)

PRACTICE QUESTION 40

> You are advised to spend about 45 minutes on this section.
> Write in full sentences.
> You are reminded of the need to plan your answer.
> You should leave enough time to check your work at the end.

Your school newspaper has asked for entries into its creative writing competition.

EITHER: Write a description as suggested by this picture.

OR: Write the opening to a short story about change.

24 marks for content and organisation
16 marks for technical accuracy
(40 marks)

41

PRACTICE QUESTION 41

You are advised to spend about 45 minutes on this section.
Write in full sentences.
You are reminded of the need to plan your answer.
You should leave enough time to check your work at the end.

Your headteacher has asked for examples of creative writing to show off on parents' evening.

EITHER: Write a short story as suggested by this picture.

OR: Write a description about feeling lost.

24 marks for content and organisation
16 marks for technical accuracy
(40 marks)

PRACTICE QUESTION 42

You are advised to spend about 45 minutes on this section.
Write in full sentences.
You are reminded of the need to plan your answer.
You should leave enough time to check your work at the end.

A regional literary magazine is searching for examples of creative writing.

EITHER: Write a description as suggested by this picture.

OR: Write a short story about feeling afraid.

24 marks for content and organisation
16 marks for technical accuracy
(40 marks)

PRACTICE QUESTION 43

You are advised to spend about 45 minutes on this section.
Write in full sentences.
You are reminded of the need to plan your answer.
You should leave enough time to check your work at the end.

Your school has asked for writing submissions for its end of term newsletter.

EITHER: Write a description as suggested by this picture.

OR: Write the opening to a story that begins: "It was now or never."

24 marks for content and organisation
16 marks for technical accuracy
(40 marks)

PRACTICE QUESTION 44

You are advised to spend about 45 minutes on this section.
Write in full sentences.
You are reminded of the need to plan your answer.
You should leave enough time to check your work at the end.

A local writing group is looking for new examples of creative writing.

EITHER: Write a description as suggested by this picture.

OR: Write the opening to a story about a challenge.

24 marks for content and organisation
16 marks for technical accuracy
(40 marks)

45

PRACTICE QUESTION 45

You are advised to spend about 45 minutes on this section.
Write in full sentences.
You are reminded of the need to plan your answer.
You should leave enough time to check your work at the end.

Your teacher has asked you to produce some creative writing for the classroom display.

EITHER: Write a description as suggested by this picture.

OR: Write the opening to a story that begins: "I had a lot on my mind."

24 marks for content and organisation
16 marks for technical accuracy
(40 marks)

PRACTICE QUESTION 46

You are advised to spend about 45 minutes on this section.
Write in full sentences.
You are reminded of the need to plan your answer.
You should leave enough time to check your work at the end.

Your school is looking for creative writing submissions for its termly literary newsletter.

EITHER: Write a short story as suggested by this picture.

OR: Write a description about a fun place.

24 marks for content and organisation
16 marks for technical accuracy
(40 marks)

PRACTICE QUESTION 47

You are advised to spend about 45 minutes on this section.
Write in full sentences.
You are reminded of the need to plan your answer.
You should leave enough time to check your work at the end.

A global writing publication has asked for samples of creative writing from students.

EITHER: Write a description as suggested by this picture.

OR: Write the opening to a story about a dangerous situation.

24 marks for content and organisation
16 marks for technical accuracy
(40 marks)

48

PRACTICE QUESTION 48

You are advised to spend about 45 minutes on this section.
Write in full sentences.
You are reminded of the need to plan your answer.
You should leave enough time to check your work at the end.

Your school has asked for writing submissions for its end of term newsletter.

EITHER: Write a description as suggested by this picture.

OR: Write the opening to a story about a family.

24 marks for content and organisation
16 marks for technical accuracy
(40 marks)

49

PRACTICE QUESTION 49

You are advised to spend about 45 minutes on this section.
Write in full sentences.
You are reminded of the need to plan your answer.
You should leave enough time to check your work at the end.

A website has asked for contributions to its writing section.

EITHER: Write a description as suggested by this picture.

OR: Write the opening to a story about a day out.

24 marks for content and organisation
16 marks for technical accuracy
(40 marks)

PRACTICE QUESTION 50

You are advised to spend about 45 minutes on this section.
Write in full sentences.
You are reminded of the need to plan your answer.
You should leave enough time to check your work at the end.

A local writing group are looking for pieces of creative writing to showcase at the town hall.

EITHER: Write the opening to a short story as suggested by this picture.

OR: Write a description about a strange experience.

24 marks for content and organisation
16 marks for technical accuracy
(40 marks)

ACKNOWLEDGEMENTS

The images used in this book are licensed for commercial use.

Every image used was sourced from one of the following:

Midjourney AI, v5.2 *(midjourney.com)*
Canva *(www.canva.com)*
Pexels *(www.pexels.com)*
Jordan Watson

Thank you for purchasing this revision guide; I hope you have found it helpful. If you did, I would be hugely grateful if you could leave a positive review on the Amazon product page so that others may be able to benefit from it too.

If you are looking for revision videos on a wide range of English-related topics and beyond, visit my YouTube channel:
youtube.com/EnglishWithWatson

If you would like to connect with me on social media, please find links to my professional profiles below:

Instagram – *instagram.com/EnglishWithWatson*
Facebook – *facebook.com/EnglishWithWatson*
Patreon – *patreon.com/EnglishWithWatson*
LinkedIn – *www.linkedin.com/in/mr-jordan-watson*